Guidelines for Learning Resource Services in Further and Higher Education

Performance and resourcing

SIXTH EDITION

Edited by

Kathy Ennis

for the Colleges of Further and Higher Education Group
of The Library Association

LIBRARY ASSOCIATION PUBLISHING
LONDON

Published by
Library Association Publishing
7 Ridgmount Street
London WC1E 7AE

Library Association Publishing is wholly owned by The Library Association.

First published 1965
Second edition 1971
Third edition 1982
Fourth edition 1990
Fifth edition 1995
This sixth edition 2000

British Library Cataloguing in Publication Data

A catalogue record for this book is available from the British Library.

ISBN 1-85604-245-6

Typeset in Garamond and Humanist 521 from author's disk by Library Association Publishing.
Printed and made in Great Britain by MPG Books Ltd, Bodmin, Cornwall.

Contents

Acknowledgments

My first, and warmest, thanks go to the *Guidelines* revision working party: Ann Edmunds, Kate Gardner, Roddie Shepherd, Shirley Ward, and Lin Watson. I thank them not only for their contributions to the text (which I think are excellent), but also to my well-being when the going got tough! I would also like to thank those people who took the time and trouble to read, comment on and even rewrite sections: Helen Ashton, Jeff Cooper, Madeleine Coyle, Stephen Gregory, Chris Kelland, David Sharp and the whole CoFHE Committee.

In the end this document is the sum of the knowledge and experience of people working within learning resource management and I am positive that it will prove an invaluable tool to others in the field.

Foreword

It gives me great pleasure to add a foreword to this new edition of *Guidelines for Learning Resource Services in Further and Higher Education* - the CoFHE *Guidelines*. Nor is it the first time that I have been associated with the *Guidelines* - having contributed to the revision of a previous edition when I myself was a College Librarian (as they were known then!) and a CoFHE activist.

From my present perspective, I am mindful that amongst the core purposes of The Library Association as reflected in its Royal Charter are:

- To promote and encourage the maintenance of adequate and appropriate provision of library and information services . . . throughout the United Kingdom, the Channel Islands and the Isle of Man.
- To promote the better management of library and information services.

And that is exactly what these *Guidelines* are about. That they are now in their sixth edition is tribute to their undoubted usefulness in helping LA members contribute to the fulfilment of these purposes within further and higher education.

Congratulations to Kathy Ennis and her team for bringing the *Guidelines* into the new millennium.

Dr Bob McKee
Chief Executive
The Library Association

Preface

Managing and developing library and learning resources services in further and higher education has never been more challenging, more important and more exciting. Libraries and learning centres have a crucial and pervasive role to play in providing a high-quality teaching and learning environment as a whole within our institutions.

The importance of libraries should be emphasized in the learning and teaching strategies developed by our colleges and universities. We actively facilitate all types of learning: curriculum-related learning; independent learning; group learning; and distributed learning. Uniquely, the modern 'hybrid' library provides access to collections, PCs and electronic resources, study places and supportive staff. We teach the core information skills necessary for academic work and learning throughout life. We are the 'hub' for distributing services off campus. We are committed to promoting literacy and IT literacy. Many libraries also provide learning development services and other important learning functions.

At the same time, our institutions and various official bodies require us to demonstrate quality and performance, to benchmark services and make self-assessments, and to show value for money and accountability. These pressures go beyond the requirements of central government, funding bodies and quality assurance agencies: they are also driven by our professional commitment to achieving high standards both in teaching and learning support and in the management and delivery of information.

This is the context within which this new edition of the *Guidelines* has been produced. Firstly, it constitutes a manual for service management and development in the new and challenging environment of post-16 lifelong learning. Secondly, it points to sources of information on strategic planning, space management, LRC design, collection development, financial management, sources of comparative statistics and other aspects of service provision and development. Finally, it provides useful information for promoting library services within the competitive financial environment within which we operate.

I commend the *Guidelines* to you. This volume will prove an invaluable part of your professional and managerial toolkit for meeting new challenges, for embracing important opportunities, and for ensuring that our libraries play their full role in the emerging Learning Age.

Professor Andrew McDonald
Director of Information Services, University of Sunderland
Chair, The Library Association Academic and Research Libraries Committee

Part 1
Introduction

1.1 Learning resource services: redefining the academic library

The academic library is one of the institution's principal educational resources. It exists to support the information needs of all members of the institution; students, teachers, managers and support staff. It provides resources in many formats. It provides the support that users need to plan, locate, retrieve, select, appraise, organize, record and communicate information. It serves the educational process as a learning centre and as an information centre, and can support the institution best when closely integrated into the academic process. It is an organization that facilitates the interaction between people and the information they need.

In recent years changes in teaching and learning methods, the move towards resource-based and flexible learning, the call for a more student-centred approach to learning, greater accountability and the inspection process have all caused senior managers of academic institutions to redefine the role of their libraries.

One of the implications of this redefinition is that many academic libraries are now part of a converged service. Either the library has acquired more functions or it has been subsumed into a much larger department. These converged services are often called 'learning resources'. The nomenclature is diverse, as is the combination of services that converge to form a learning resource service: for example, library, media resources, reprographics, ICT/ILT, careers, guidance, counselling. Indeed, some managers of learning resource services may now be responsible not only for the resourcing of curriculum areas but also for curriculum delivery and consequently for the line management of full and part-time teaching staff.

These *Guidelines* address the quality, resource and service issues of a learning resource service whilst recognizing that the reality of such a service is enormously varied and that there is no definitive model.

Throughout the following text, the generic term 'learning resource service' has been used to encompass a range of scenarios.

1.2　Defining the role of a learning resource service

A learning resource service has a number of interlinked roles to provide an effective learning environment. These include:

- the provision and interpretation of information, knowledge and resources to support student learning
- the provision of facilities and a suitable atmosphere to enable students to learn at their own pace, either individually or in a group, at times appropriate to themselves
- the provision and delivery of information skills programmes
- the provision of facilities and materials to support academic staff in delivering the curriculum
- the provision of information and materials to assist senior managers to make informed decisions relating to the institution as a whole

Other roles might include: providing facilities such as word-processing and binding to enable students to prepare work for submission; contributing to the educational and cultural life of the local community by mounting exhibitions or conferences; providing an archive service for the institution; or providing a careers service.

The ultimate role of the learning resource service will depend on which services have been converged and where the greater emphasis lies. For example, a convergence of library and ICT/ILT services will give an information focus, whereas the convergence of library, ICT/ILT with basic skills support, counselling and guidance will tend to give a student support emphasis.

Part 2
Performance

2.1 Strategic management

In simple terms strategic management can be described as:

> a plan of action to enable an organisation to move from where it is now to where it wants to be at a future date. Managers need to have an idea about where they want the organisation to be in the future and the route it is going to follow to get there.'[1]

Strategic management is also about anticipating changes in the external environment and developing a service so that it retains and enhances its effectiveness and relevance.

A means of ensuring that a service can adapt to change while continuing to operate effectively is for that service to work within a quality framework.

2.2 A quality framework

Quality is hard to define but everyone can recognize it. To measure the quality of a service or demonstrate it in quantitative terms is notoriously difficult. The standard definition of quality, which is often cited, is that of 'fitness for purpose'.

To enable the fitness for purpose of a learning resource service to be assessed a number of factors must be present. They are:

- a quality policy
- a statement of mission and aims of the learning resource service which stem from the mission and aims of the institution
- a process of systematic strategic planning
- a means of measuring needs and satisfaction levels of users
- a means of relating learning resources policies to the needs and wishes of users
- a review mechanism based on internal evaluation and external inspection or assessment.

2.2.1 Quality policy

A quality policy document is the record of the systems and procedures that are in place to ensure that users have a satisfactory experience and that quality continues to improve.

A quality policy must specify:

- the aims and objectives of the service
- the procedures for monitoring the delivery of those aims and objectives.

It must include:

- a manual or documentation of procedures
- mechanisms for collecting data to evaluate effectiveness
- a feedback loop to ensure that identified weaknesses are dealt with.

It must also indicate:

- a culture which stresses that quality is the responsibility of all staff.

Many quality systems exist such as ISO 9000, Total Quality Management (TQM), Investors in People (IIP), target setting and peer assessment or accreditation. Learning resource managers must decide which method best suits the needs of their own institution. Whatever system is used will need to match that used by the parent institution and meet the requirements of any inspecting, awarding or validating bodies.

2.2.2 Mission

Like any business the learning resource service needs a clearly defined mission in order to focus its work and to assist forward planning.

Mission statements vary but they should all describe the learning resource service's basic purpose, derived from the parent institution's mission statement, and relate to the institution's organizational structure.

A typical statement might be:

To provide an innovative, responsive and proactive learning resource service supporting the learning, teaching, and research needs of the user community, in such a way as to meet its requirements and expectations and achieve the highest professional standards in a cost effective, stimulating and user friendly manner.

The formulation of a mission statement is a group activity. Therefore the learning resource service mission statement should be developed with the cooperation of all learning resource service staff and not be written independently by the manager of the service.

2.2.3 Aims

The aims of the learning resource service should be formulated in a process of consultation between the services' staff, its users, the academic board and senior management. The aims should reflect the mission statements of the institution and the learning resource service.

A typical statement of aims might be:

- *to identify and provide access to the learning resource services required to support the learning, teaching and research activities of the institution*
- *to manage those resources efficiently, effectively and economically*
- *to establish an environment conducive to study and which caters for multiple learning styles and for individual and group learning*
- *to liaise with boards of study or course committees and students to establish their requirements and to cooperate with management and other support services to meet these needs*
- *to teach users about the learning resource service facilities and to develop their information skills*
- *to maintain effective links with staff of the institution in order to understand and, where necessary, respond to changes in education, approaches to learning, and corporate policy.*

Aims cannot be static. They should be regularly reviewed and amended in the light of alterations in the mission statements and by referral to the relevant performance standards.

It is essential that when institutional policy documents are being drafted or revised, their impact on the learning resource service should be considered, and resource implications be taken into account. Such institutional documents might include policy statements, strategic or marketing plans, student charters and contracts, codes of conduct and grievance and disciplinary procedures.

2.2.4 Objectives

Objectives are more specific than aims. They are the outcomes that satisfy the aims, and they must be measurable and achievable within resource and time constraints.

For example, if the aim is:

to establish an environment conducive to study and which caters for multiple learning styles and for individual and group learning

then the objectives might include:

- *the identification of the balance between individual and group study requirements*
- *the provision of appropriate ICT/ILT*
- *the staffing requirements.*

Objectives should be set in such terms that it is possible to measure their fulfilment against service standards, performance measures, indicators and benchmarks.

2.2.5 Planning

Planning is an integrated process of making decisions by bringing together a series of ideas so that they can relate to each other and form a rational whole to establish the action to be taken.

A strategic plan charts what is to be achieved, while an operational plan determines how it is to be achieved. The strategic plan of a learning resource service will be drawn up as part of the planning cycle of the institution. It should be based on analytical evidence, for example, statistical data, benchmarking data, or a SWOT analysis of the service.

Before operational planning can begin, an evaluation of the existing service, and an analysis of how it fits with other services in the institution, needs to be undertaken in order to determine where improvements can or need to be made.

The operational plan is a time-dependent subset of the strategic plan, constructed from the identified objectives and targets.

Both the strategic and operational plans of the learning resource service relate directly to the parent institution's development or strategic plan, and are informed by the learning resource service's mission, aims, objectives and targets.

2.2.6 Targets and action plans

Targets are the most specific part of the strategic management process. They form what is often called the 'action plan'. Targets are essential for the control of tasks, and the achievement of objectives.

For example, if the objective is:

the provision of appropriate ICT/ILT

the action plan might consist of the following targets:

- *to complete a survey of the ICT/ILT needs of learning resources users by [date]*
- *to determine the order of priority of these ICT/ILT needs by [date]*
- *to produce a cost-benefit analysis of additional ICT/ILT needs by [date].*

The action plan must set a date for completion and individual responsibility to each target.

By identifying achievable objectives and allocating targets, an operational plan is developed.

Once the targets are met and the objectives achieved, the operational plan is complete.

2.2.7 Performance measurement

Performance measures are used to gauge how well a service fulfils its purpose. Despite considerable debate about performance indicators there remains no universally accepted set of measures that can be used to evaluate learning resource services in academic institutions.

Deciding what to measure is difficult but should always be related to the aims and objectives of the parent organization and thence to the purpose of the service being measured. Streatfield and Markless in their report *The effective college library*[2] noted:

> performance indicators and targets . . . should be cast in college priority terms
> and seek to make the . . . contribution to college development explicit.

In deciding what to measure it is vital to consider the purpose of the measurements being collected. They can be used to aid the effective management of the learning resource service and to demonstrate the contribution of the service to the institution as a whole.

Performance indicators cannot remain static. They will need to change over time and will need continual evaluation in order to ensure their relevance to current issues within the learning resource service, the institution of which it forms a part and the wider educational sphere.

Measurements can be split into two main types:

- quantitative data, such as annual issues or expenditure per full-time equivalent (FTE) and
- qualitative data, such as self-assessment reports, feedback forms and focus groups (see Appendix 3).

Management data form the basis from which performance measures can be derived, and as such should be as efficient, consistent and as reliable as possible. The Library Association's Professional Adviser (Academic) has produced a comprehensive management data checklist of performance measures that may prove useful. (See Appendix 3.)

Performance measurement is an essential management tool, which aids planning and helps justify the service. It is not merely a tool for operational management but a stimulus to strategic planning.

2.2.8 Benchmarking and comparative data

Benchmarking provides useful sources of evidence for evaluating learning resource services.

Benchmarking is often described as a method of comparing like with like. It has two elements:

- the comparison of key data obtained from similar institutions
- the comparison of systems, that is, how things are done, within similar institutions.

It is thus particularly useful in assessing performance, as there is a danger, when comparing figures alone, of not taking into account the different approaches and parameters within which each service operates.

Comparative data sources tend to be numerically based. Examples include:

- *Library and learning resource services in further education: the report of the 1996/97 survey*[3]
- the SCONUL annual library statistics
- HCLRG statistics
- UK HE library management statistics (SCONUL/HCLRG).

2.2.9   Users

In evaluating any learning resource service, it is vital to ensure that users of all types remain the focal point of any evaluation. Users of academic learning resource services are not a homogenous group; they include students, distance learners, teaching and support staff, researchers and external users.

Students are not a single group; different types of students have different needs. They depend on factors such as academic level, mode of attendance, location, age, disability, language and methods of teaching and learning.

There is no 'typical student' and therefore no easily agreed description of what a student needs from a learning resource service.

Staff, too, have varying needs and requirements. The needs of the managers of an institution will be very different from those of teaching and support staff.

External users can include local business people, distance learners, school children, members of the general public, Ufi students, Open University students and students from other colleges or institutions.

Any system of quality measurement must consider all users and try to meet their needs wherever possible. It is also vital to consider non-users and to try to ascertain why potential users do not use the service.

Many issues can influence user satisfaction levels:

- resources
  - the number, range and format of the learning resources should be sufficient to meet the learning, teaching and research needs of students and staff
  - the learning resources should be well organized and maintained in strict order
  - the building, facilities and materials should be appropriate for their purpose.
- atmosphere and ambience
  - the service should be open at times convenient to most users
  - the atmosphere should be welcoming and friendly
  - all areas should be clean and tidy
  - the facilities should be visible, easy to use and clearly signed
  - there should be a comfortable working environment where users feel personally secure.

- service credibility and reliability
  - the service should be seen to contain current information and have appropriate older material available
  - the staff should provide appropriate help and advice
  - the service should be reliable, dependable and efficient.
- staff
  - the staff should be polite, attentive and friendly
  - the staff should be able to communicate effectively
  - the staff should be able to gauge the needs of users.

This list does not attempt to be comprehensive but indicates some of the factors that influence user satisfaction levels.

The means of gathering user information include surveys, questionnaires, feedback forms, focus groups, user groups and committees, and comments and suggestions from individuals, course teams, committees or other forms of institutional evaluation. The information gathered should then be used to form the basis of a service charter, a set of service standards or a service level agreement.

2.2.10   Inspection and assessment

A crucial element of the quality approach is the ability to demonstrate the provision of a quality service. This can best be achieved by a mixture of inspection, evaluation and assessment.

2.2.10.1   Internal inspection and peer assessment

All organizations need to have internal inspection or validation procedures in addition to such external procedures as may exist. Procedures such as SWOT analysis, action planning, target setting and performance measurement can be used.

However, it is often difficult for those directly responsible for a service to stand back and evaluate provision objectively. Learning resource managers may wish to invite other people, either from within their own institution, or fellow professionals from other institutions, to carry out evaluations.

Learning resource services in further education and sixth form colleges may choose to use the CoLRIC Peer Accreditation Scheme, which uses trained assessors, to assess learning resource services and award a grade to that service. The Scheme uses a five-tier rating system based on the ability to fulfil a number of criteria, which are either mandatory, core or supportive. A certificate is awarded to services that achieve excellence.

Other local schemes exist. In the Merseyside region, for example, the Circle of Merseyside College Librarians also has a peer evaluation scheme available for the learning resource services of further education and sixth form colleges.

Whatever method is used, self-assessment will generally form an essential part of any formal inspection or validation process.

2.2.10.2   External inspection and assessment

Inspections of learning resources in further and higher education are carried out by a number of bodies, for example:

- FEFC/HEFCE/Estyn (Wales)/DENI (Northern Ireland)/QAA/OFSTED/Her Majesty's Inspectorate (Scotland)
- Franchising bodies
- Awarding bodies (eg Edexcel, C&G, AAT, IPD)
- ISO 9000 validating bodies
- IIP awarding bodies.

During inspections learning resource services will find that they are assessed as part of the inspections of individual subject areas and of cross-college services and facilities.

Guidelines exist for both higher and further education inspections. SCONUL has produced an *Aide-memoire for assessors when evaluating library and computing services*,[4] which acts as an adjunct to HEFCE's *Assessors' handbook*[5] and which has the full backing of HCLRG, SCONUL and UCISA. It is given to all assessors to aid them on their Teaching Quality Assessment (TQA) visits and can also prove a useful and valuable tool in preparing for such a visit.

The FEFC has guidance notes for inspectors and CoLRIC has produced *Guidelines for inspection of college libraries/learning resource services*.[6]

Inspections, validations and accreditation visits usually seek to evaluate the quality of the learning resource provision by finding evidence and information regarding the following aspects:

- management and planning
    - the remit of the learning resource service within the institution's strategic plan and mission statement
    - the position of the learning resource service within the institution's structure
    - the perceived professional identity and responsibilities of the learning resource staff
    - the procedures for establishing the learning resource budget.
- organizational structure
    - how the learning resource service is organized, including the grading of staff
    - systems for liaising with other departments within the institution
    - integration of learning resources into curriculum delivery.
- learning resource provision
    - the types of services and facilities provided
    - the level of service provision for stock, equipment, study space etc
    - comparison against agreed benchmarks.
- quality assurance
    - the systems that exist to collect relevant information on performance
    - evidence that weaknesses are recognized and dealt with.
- feedback from users and potential users
    - evidence from users and potential users of the service as to how well the service satisfies their needs.

There has been much concern about the way inspections are carried out, particularly in further education, where learning resource services are not graded separately but form part of general resources, which include catering, crèche facilities and accommodation. A particular concern is that inspectors have little or no experience or expertise in learning resource provision and do not understand or value the contribution of learning resources. It is the responsibility of learning resource managers and staff in all types of institution to do all they can by the use of detailed self-assessment, peer appraisal and internal inspection to rectify this situation.

At national level it is the responsibility of bodies and groups such The Library Association, CoFHE, UC&R, CoLRIC, HCLRG and SCONUL to make the case for quality assurance and inspection systems which recognize the centrality of learning and information resources to quality in learning, teaching and research. These bodies also have a role to play in contributing to the development of such systems.

The case is pursued by contact with quality assurance and inspection bodies, planning and funding agencies, central government and other national sector bodies.

The continued development of resource-based learning, ICT/ILT mediated learning and independent learning add force to the case for adequate quality assurance arrangements for learning resource provision.

2.3   Promotion of the service

An essential part of the quality approach to service provision is marketing. Promotion is at the heart of marketing.

The public service approach has been criticized for tending to adopt a 'take it or leave it' attitude. Too often it is assumed that, as users will benefit from the services provided, they will make the effort to discover what services are available and make use of them.

However, marketing textbooks identify six stages of customer behaviour, which emphasize the necessity of promoting a service:

- lack of awareness of product or service
- awareness of product or service
- interest in product or service
- desire for product or service
- conviction about value of product or service
- purchase or adoption of product or service.

Learning resource managers must ensure that users can identify each of the services available from the learning resource service. This can be done in a variety of ways, for example:

- including an entry about learning resource services in the institutional handbook, and on the website and intranet
- producing leaflets or guides to specific services
- including information in course leaflets
- ensuring that relevant information, and supporting documentation, is given during general induction sessions
- ensuring that relevant information is available in large print and audio format to inform the visually and hearing impaired, and in languages other than English as appropriate
- developing strong links with teaching departments.

These methods should assist the learning resource manager to develop awareness of, interest in, desire for and conviction about the value of learning resource services amongst students and staff.

References

1   Hannagan, T, *Management: concepts and practices*, Financial Times Management, 1998.
2   Streatfield, D and Markless, S, *The effective college library*, FEDA, 1997.
3   Wallace, W and Marsden, D, *Library and learning resource services in further education: the report of the 1996/97 survey commissioned by The Library Association*, The Survey and Statistical Research Centre, Sheffield Hallam University, 1999.
4   Standing Conference of National and University Libraries, *Aide-memoire for assessors when evaluating library and computing services*, SCONUL, 1996.

5   Higher Education Funding Council for England: Quality Assessment Division, *Assessor's handbook*, HEFCE, 1996.

6   Council for Learning Resources in Colleges, *Guidelines for inspection of college libraries/learning resource services*, CoLRIC, 1993.

Part 3
Resourcing

3.1   The learning environment

The aim of learning resource staff should be to create a welcoming learning environment, available and accessible to all the institution's staff and students, well organized for information provision and conducive to a variety of patterns of learning activity such as quiet study, group work, seminar work, workshops or presentations.

Regulations from government departments and funding bodies about various aspects of the learning resource environment should be adhered to and regular assessment of these aspects of provision should take place.

3.1.1   Range of accommodation

It is not possible to make generalizations about the physical scope or pattern of learning resource provision within institutions. Accommodation will be located in a variety of different physical settings depending on the institutional learning contexts and the historical decisions about locations.

Many scenarios can be envisaged: a single large university or college learning resource service on several floors of a building; one or more large flexible study centres with library and ICT/ILT facilities; several smaller resource centres, in some cases attached to subject departments; or a traditional library, more or less separated from other types of learning or ICT/ILT workshops.

An institution may have many sites, near or far; each may be autonomous or be networked to a central site, and each may have its own learning resource centre, library or flexible learning workshop with differing functions and patterns of management. Learning resources may be a converged service within an institution but not necessarily combined physically in the same building.

3.1.2   Allocation of space

In *Guidance on floorspace management in further education colleges: supplement to circular 97/37*[1] the FEFC recommends that the total area for further education college learning resource centres: 'should comprise at least 10% of total college area . . . and should include computer resources which may be flexibly used for teaching or learning'.

Another way of describing this recommendation is that the minimum area for further education learning resource centres should be the equivalent of 20% of the total teaching space.

An alternative recommendation from the FEFC and the DfEE (*Accommodation for changes in further education: design note 50*)[2] is to consider the proportion of 'learning space' in further education colleges. The emerging pattern is for learning space, that is, space appropriate for student-centred or resource-based learning, to be allocated the same space as general and specialized teaching areas such as laboratories or engineering workshops. Each of these areas might take up 20% of the total college area, but in practice these ratios are blurred because some computer areas are used for teaching, learning and open-access functions.

Thus the proportion of space allocated to different areas of a college might be as follows:

- 20% general teaching space
- 20% specialized teaching space
- 20% learning space
- 40% general and administrative facilities such as a refectory, reception areas and finance office.

Learning resource managers are advised to consider the spatial recommendations made in *FEFC Circular 97/37*[3] in particular. They are minimum requirements and can be used to calculate the recommended learning resource accommodation at their own institutions.

In addition to spatial requirements, other factors need to be taken into account:

- convergence: as more functions are incorporated into the learning resource centre the amount of space per student will need to be increased; for example, ICT/ILT and audiovisual equipment make a proportionately greater demand on space
- flexible or resource based learning methods: an increased emphasis on these teaching methods is likely to increase the amount of time students spend in learning resource centres and therefore puts more pressure on space
- the increasing amount of group study work as a curriculum requirement
- part-time students: a higher proportion of part-time students increases space needs – FTE student numbers do not indicate the number of bodies in a room!
- students or staff with physical disabilities: these users must have equal access.

3.1.3 Use of space within learning resource centres

The essential feature of this type of accommodation is that it is available and accessible for student and staff information needs.

Wherever learning materials and information services are provided there should be adequate space for:

- users to retrieve both paper-based and electronic learning materials and information
- suitable storage for all types of learning materials
- users to circulate freely
- individuals and small groups of users to work and study quietly
- learning resource staff to assist and train individuals and groups in searching for information
- learning resource staff to operate issue and enquiry desks
- learning resource staff to have their own work space.

The SCONUL briefing paper *Space requirements for academic libraries and learning resource centres*[4] is a discussion on the space requirements of higher education learning resource services. It makes three practical suggestions to combat problems associated with space, recommending a flexible, but focused, space management initiative:

- convert storage space to seating space by using high density storage systems

- use radical stock disposal policies to create more space
- extend opening hours to allow students greater access.

3.1.4   Design and layout in learning resource centres

A number of design principles are highlighted in another CoFHE publication, *Library design*.[5] These form a good starting point when considering the design of learning resource centres:

- design from the inside out: think about the activities that need to take place in a learning resource centre before the need for it to fit into a certain shape
- design for purpose: how many users? which services? what kind of stock?
- design for changing needs: flexibility is important
- look out for hazards in building plans if designing a new learning resource centre
- group noisy activities, use screening or furnishings to shelter quiet areas.

Designing or altering the internal layout of a learning resource centre is constrained by the space available. But there are several other factors to consider such as:

- the shape of the building and rooms
- the position of light switches
- the accessibility of cabling and power sockets
- the number, size and position of the windows
- the size and nature of the stock and equipment
- the number of learning resource staff
- the number of potential users.

There are a variety of methods for developing design ideas. They include:

- visiting other learning resource centres
- talking to other learning resource managers to find out how they solved problems in their institution
- contacting The Library Association's Professional Adviser (Academic) for suggestions of examples of good practice and innovative design
- scanning building or architectural magazines.

An interesting and useful article on design, in *Belfast 96: designs on learning*,[6] a collection of CoFHE conference papers, describes the results of a questionnaire and interviews with users about what they would like to find in a learning resource centre. Users wanted a social space to meet others 'who know the answers'; they wanted a choice of quiet, group and noisy study areas close to a variety of learning materials; they wanted an integrated workspace including access to ICT/ILT; they wanted learning resource staff to be visible and accessible. All this and an open and attractive environment too!

Learning resource centres are people-oriented environments. Therefore certain design features are essential such as comfortable seating, some natural as well as artificial light, the attractive use of colour in decoration and suitable acoustics.

3.1.5   Inclusiveness

The term 'inclusiveness' refers to targeted or under-represented groups, for example, those on low incomes or the unemployed, ethnic minorities, people with learning difficulties or disabilities, mature students, and young people with behavioural difficulties.

These groups will increasingly form the post compulsory student population. Catering for the needs of such a diverse group will have an impact on the interior design of buildings, which will in turn have an impact on the design of learning resource centres.

The set of key questions listed in the FEDA Report *Equality assurance*[7] are a useful tool in assessing whether a learning resource centre is accessible to a wide variety of users.

3.1.6   Equipment

The following is a list of equipment that could usefully be provided as part of a learning resource service. Other equipment may also be necessary depending on the range of services offered:

- furniture and shelving
    - ergonomic study spaces, service points and office furniture
    - flexible shelving systems
    - display equipment.
- communications
    - telephone
    - fax
    - e-mail.
- security systems
    - stock security system
    - secure staff work space.
- automation
    - management system for operations control and monitoring
    - network access to the institution's academic and administrative networks
    - computing facilities for learning resource service staff, including Internet access.
- ICT/ILT
    - multimedia workstations for users, including Internet access
    - CD-ROM and DVD.
- audiovisual technology
    - video and audio tape playback equipment
    - OHP and OHP/LCD projection panel
    - slide viewing equipment.
- reprographic
    - photocopier (including colour)
    - scanner
    - printer.

3.1.7   Health and safety

Learning resource managers must be familiar with current health and safety legislation including the Workplace (Health, Safety and Welfare) Regulations, 1992. Familiarity and compliance with institutional health and safety policies and procedures will also be required. As employees, line managers and custodians of spaces open to staff, students and members of the public, learning resource managers will experience different roles and responsibilities in the maintenance of a healthy and safe environment.

The Management of Health and Safety at Work Regulations 1992, and the amendments of 1994, require all employers to assess all hazards present within the workplace, together with their associated levels of risk. Assessment of workplace hazards and risks should encompass provisions and stipulations within current health and safety regulations. For example, Manual Handling Operation Regulations 1992, Health and Safety (Display Screen Equipment) Regulations 1992, and Control of Substances Hazardous to Health Regulations (COSHH) 1994 may all have implications for learning resource service managers and staff.

Risk assessments need not be undertaken by a 'safety expert' but must be completed to 'adequate' or 'suitable and sufficient' levels. Elements of risk assessment may therefore be delegated to service or line managers. Having completed a risk assessment, steps must be taken to remove or minimize risk of injury or ill health from significant hazards. It is important to document the findings of risk assessment inspections and also to record the follow-up actions. Risk assessments should be reviewed when it is suspected that previous assessments are no longer valid. Planning for, and embarking on special projects (eg stock relocation or reorganization), may also require risk assessments together with follow-up actions to minimize or remove any suspected significant hazards and risks.

Learning resource centres have developed as welcoming and informal places where the emphasis is on good access for users; inevitably there will be conflict between these principles and the imposition of rules and regulations for security. However, the value of stock and IT equipment makes security a necessary consideration. A reasonable level of staffing and supervision will deter thefts, and clear sight-lines from learning resource service staff desks are essential for the prevention of antisocial behaviour.

At least three aspects of security, affecting learning resource service staff, should be considered according to *DfEE Design Note 50.*[8]

- ever increasing numbers of users of college buildings, both from within and without, require monitoring and supervision; learning resource service staff may be vulnerable if working in the evening or at weekends when parts of the building may be quiet and unattended
- learning resource centres with expensive stock and equipment are vulnerable to theft: a balance has to be kept between making them accessible and pilfer-proof
- money handling is also a security risk for learning resource service staff, particularly during non-standard working hours.

Possible ways of achieving some degree of protection for staff include using personal alarms, surveillance cameras, CCTV or mirrors, emergency telephone numbers and even security staff.

Learning resource staff should be aware of institutional policies and any associated documentation such as student charters or contracts, codes of conduct, grievance and disciplinary procedures. Any discipline problems in the learning resource centre should be dealt with in accordance with these policies and with the support of the appropriate line manager.

3.1.8   Reports and assessment

FEFC Circular 97/12[9] includes learning resource centres under the heading 'Cross-college /general provision'. The self-assessment criteria stipulate that: 'general facilities to support learning, including libraries and learning resource centres, are of an appropriate quality and readily accessible to students'.

Indicative sources of evidence required by the Council to validate the assessment are: 'the quality of the learning environment, including the amount and use made of the space available to students'.

Recent FEFC Inspection reports for various colleges have commented on the use of learning resource service accommodation, its attractiveness and accessibility. Layouts to support varied learning styles and students with disabilities are praised, while the number of study spaces and the provision of ICT/ILT facilities have been scrutinized carefully.

3.1.9   Planning for the future

It has already been stated that one ideal is to produce a flexible learning environment which can respond to change. It is obviously difficult to predict what may develop in five years' time, particularly in relation to ICT/ILT and the curriculum.

The current FEFC vision for colleges, as expressed in *Networking lifelong learning: an ILT development strategy for FE*,[10] is a networked learning environment supporting internal and distance learners: wide and local area networks, one Internet-enabled PC per five student users at peak times, with learning materials available on the institution's intranet.

Institutions are increasingly providing large flexible study centres that are open all the year round and provide access to ICT/ILT and the Internet. It will be up to learning resource managers to ensure that their study centres are flexible enough to be incorporated into this vision and not marginalized as a traditional but out-of-date learning environment.

One interesting new approach is to consider using scenario planning as a way of not merely forecasting trends but also recognizing and adapting to change. The idea is to construct two to four scenarios growing logically from the current situation; the resulting visions are then sold to the senior management team of the institution. This is a technique that learning resource managers could use to clarify alternative ways forward. A discussion of this method can be found in an article in the *Library Association Record* of June 1999, 'First find some visionaries',[11] by Antony Brewerton.

3.2 Staff

Learning resource staff make a core contribution to learning, teaching and research in further and higher education. They are responsible for supplying the learning and information resource and service needs of their users. They manage and operate a major educational facility and the systems established to exploit it. They make their contribution in the following areas of activity:

- managing resources for learning, information and research by maximizing access and availability: the diversity of resources including ICT/ILT is making the management of access and availability increasingly complex
- designing and managing systems of control and retrieval for resources for learning, information and research: traditionally this has meant cataloguing, classification and indexing; increasingly, it is about issues such as control of web-based resources, metadata management and large scale resource discovery
- designing and managing environments for independent learning: this involves the management and integration of physical and electronic or virtual learning environments and spaces
- mediating between learners and information seekers and learning and information resources and services: learning resources staff have a key role as learning resource mediators, as learning facilitators, as learner enablers; this contribution is crucial to the success of strategies for resource-based and ICT/ILT mediated learning
- teaching transferable information, learning and knowledge navigation skills: these are core enabling skills for independent and lifelong learning
- providing expertise and advice on the selection and acquisition of learning and information resources in learning programme and research areas
- contributing to the development and implementation of strategies for resource based and distributed learning: this contribution can be, and is, made at institutional, cross-institutional, cross-sectoral and national levels.

Within this context, it is the job of learning resource staff to ensure that:

- there are sound links between the service and the academic processes of the institution ie the planning, design, delivery and assessment of learning programmes, the development of research activity
- user and institutional needs for learning and information resources are identified and addressed
- institutional management is informed of opportunities for developing the contribution of the learning resource service
- services are continually developed in line with institutional and national strategies
- learning resources environments are conducive to learning in a variety of modes and styles
- services are inclusive, and accessible to learners with a variety of needs and circumstances
- users are provided with professional enquiry and information services
- there are mechanisms for service evaluation, and quality management

- services are provided efficiently and cost-effectively
- links are maintained with the wider information world, local and national organizations, government departments and companies
- their own professional skills and knowledge are kept up-to-date.

Developments in resource-based, ICT/ILT mediated learning mean that learning resource staff should work increasingly as members of cross-professional learning and teaching teams. Many staff are required to adopt flexible work patterns in order to meet demands for enhanced access to services.

3.2.1 Status, grading and qualifications

A well resourced and professionally managed learning resource service is one of the most important facilities of any educational institution. It is also likely to be one of the largest capital assets. High calibre, well motivated and appropriately qualified and experienced staff are essential to ensure that this resource makes the fullest possible contribution to the goals of the institution. The range of services provided by the learning resource service means that an appropriate staffing structure needs to be in place, with staff appointed across a range of specialisms and skills. All posts should be graded according to the level of contribution that they make, and the level of responsibility that they bear.

Staff who are responsible for the delivery of the library and information aspect of a learning resource service should be Chartered Members of The Library Association or candidates for registration. The use of professionally qualified and Chartered Librarians is part of the quality assurance process. A Chartered Member will have:

- completed an approved course of study at graduate or postgraduate level
- undergone a period of workplace training followed by the submission of evidence of professional skills
- signed a Code of Professional Conduct (see Appendix 5) which commits them to be competent in their professional activities and to keep their skills and knowledge up-to-date
- demonstrated a commitment to continuing professional development
- involvement in a professional network which continually develops professional practice.

3.2.2 Staffing structure and roles

The head of a learning resource service should have a salary level and status on a par with senior colleagues within the institution with equivalent responsibilities. This would normally be at head of department or director level. The major areas of responsibility of the head of service include:

- contributing to the strategic planning and management of the institution as a whole
- integration of the service with all other managerial and academic components and processes of the institution

- planning, development, direction and promotion of the service
- overall management of all the resources – human, financial, physical, electronic – which comprise the service
- advising on the resource requirements of the service and preparation of budgets
- establishing and reviewing a comprehensive framework of policies, systems and procedures
- service evaluation and quality
- service cost-effectiveness
- positioning the service in the wider local, regional and national information world.

In larger institutions, members of the service's senior management team will normally share these responsibilities. Ultimate responsibility remains with the head of service.

The structure of the service and allocation of roles and responsibilities will depend on the size of the service and range of services provided. Typically the functions will include:

- academic liaison
- learner support and learning facilitation
- information/learning skills teaching
- collection management and development
- information services and systems
- document delivery, including external document delivery (interlibrary loans)
- information and enquiry services
- development of resource-based and open and distance learning materials and services
- electronic services, systems and publications
- services for users with special needs
- current awareness
- special collections
- signs, guiding and promotional literature
- front-line service delivery and supervision, for example, reception, lending services, booking systems, record updating, ICT/ILT support, rota management
- supervision of service users
- intranet/Internet management and development
- cataloguing, classification and indexing
- acquisition of learning and information resources and services
- management system maintenance and development
- team leadership/section management
- staff management, staff induction, staff development and appraisal
- financial management and control
- performance data collection and analysis
- copyright compliance
- audiovisual and media services
- technician services
- administrative and secretarial services.

The different levels of post that the structure may need to contain include: deputy head of service; service area management and planning posts; academic and subject liaison posts; user services posts; technical/ bibliographic/systems services posts; first-level professional posts; supervisory posts; front-line service delivery and user support posts; administration and ancillary posts; trainee posts.

Typical post titles include:

- senior management:
    College/University Librarian; Director of Library and Information Services; Head of Learning Resources; Learning Resources Manager/Co-ordinator/ Librarian; Learning Centres Manager/Director; Head of Learning Support Services
- second tier management:
    Deputy Librarian/Learning Resources Manager; Sub-Librarian; Assistant Director; Head of Bibliographic Services/Technical Services/Network and System Services; Head of Academic Services/Reader Services/User Services/Public Services; Campus or Site Librarian/Learning Centre Manager; Team Leader; Section Head; Library Manager; Information Services Manager; Resource Based Learning Manager; Information, Communications and Learning Technology Manager
- professional:
    Assistant Librarian; Subject Librarian; Resources Librarian; Liaison Librarian; Faculty Librarian; Learning Centre Librarian; Information Specialist/Officer/ Coordinator; Learning Resources Officer/Adviser; Curriculum Resources Officer; Curriculum Support Adviser; Learning Adviser; Information Adviser; Information Facilitator; Learning Facilitator; Senior Learning Adviser/ Librarian; Systems/Circulation/Acquisitions (or other functional area) Librarian/Manager; Cataloguer
- paraprofessional:
    Library Assistant; Learning Resources/Centre Assistant; Learning Support Assistant; Information Assistant; Clerical Assistant; Senior Library/Learning Resources Assistant, Computer Support Assistant; Technician.

3.2.3　Quantity of staff

The number of staff required will be determined by such factors as:

- the size of the institution
- the number of sites
- the style of curriculum delivery
- the range of services provided
- the requirement for access at times that are convenient to users
- the need to maintain managerial, support and developmental activities, as well as front-line service delivery
- the need to ensure the safety of staff and students, and to maintain the quality of learning environments
- the need to maintain agreed levels of service.

3.2.4   Staff development

In common with all other staff in further and higher education, there is a continuing need for learning resource service staff to develop their skills and knowledge. Staff development is essential to service quality and service development. Broad areas for skills and knowledge development appropriate for learning resource service staff include:

- learning and teaching, including learner support and learning facilitation
- strategic and operational management
- ICT/ILT
- team-working and partnership
- professional and technical skills in librarianship/learning resources management (eg cataloguing and classification, electronic and web-based resources management, enquiry and information services, subject specialist services)
- advice, guidance and counselling
- awareness of the wider policy issues affecting further and higher education and the information world.

All levels of learning resource service staff should have the opportunity to follow courses leading to appropriate qualifications, including teaching and management qualifications, and to take part in external courses, in–service training and other forms of continuing professional development (CPD). They should have access to the same practical support, including financial assistance and additional leave, as is available to colleagues in other departments. Para-professional and other clerical, technical or administrative staff should equally be encouraged to obtain appropriate qualifications, such as City and Guilds and NVQs or SVQs.

The Library Association has produced a Framework for Professional Development to encourage members to review systematically the state of their knowledge and skills. It is based on the belief that continuing professional development is a responsibility of the individual working in partnership with their employer. The document encourages librarians to analyse their needs, develop a coherent CPD programme and record progress.

Staff development and training should be considered an integral part of any staff appraisal scheme. They should cover individual needs identified through appraisal as well as institutionally driven training programmes. Conversely staff should wherever possible link their CPD activities with their appraisal schemes and with staff development programmes available within their institutions.

Learning resource staff need to maintain formal and informal contacts with others working in the profession if they are to develop their contribution to the full. By participating in professional meetings, conferences and similar activities, they will be able to keep abreast of new developments and best practice. Involvement in professional activities will also reflect prestige on the institution.

3.3   Finance

It is the learning resource manager's responsibility to advise institutional management of the learning resource service's financial needs, to prepare estimates and budgets, and to control expenditure within agreed objectives.

An analysis of the type, level and cost of the learning resource service should be carried out during the strategic planning process. The institution's expectations of that service should then be met with the provision of an appropriate level of funding.

Resource management for learning resource managers generally means:

- an annual bid, based on estimates of need and previous budgets, for funds to buy materials and to cover operating costs and ongoing costs such as service and maintenance contracts and network licence renewals
- a separate bid for capital equipment and associated maintenance costs
- periodic bids for posts to be added to the staffing establishment, or, if there are vacancies in an existing establishment, for the 'release' of the post for filling by permanent or temporary appointment
- occasional requests for more resources in other areas – most notably space
- allocation of the available resources between the various spending heads
  - payroll/non-payroll
  - materials/operating costs
  - books/journals/other media
- monitoring the rate of spend of the resources made available under each major heading in response to the various bids submitted
- production of an annual report and summary financial statement for transmission to the officers of the parent institution
- regular cost-cutting exercises, whether driven by a central directive concerning a percentage reduction in projected spend or to maintain value for money
- periodic reviews of actual and potential capacity for income generation, within or without the institution.

Learning resource staff must ensure that resources are managed, and are seen to be managed, efficiently and effectively.

When estimating the cost of the service, the following factors need to be taken into consideration:

- general overheads: lighting, heating
- staff: salaries, training costs, time spent in specific activities
- curriculum demands and developments: levels of study, teaching and learning styles, student numbers, different disciplines and taught hours
- number of sites: duplication of equipment and materials
- materials purchase: new and replacement stock, periodical subscriptions, lost material
- furniture, fittings, equipment: developments in educational technology, requirements of learners with special needs, security systems, damage, wear and tear
- maintenance of equipment: depreciation, loss, upgrading
- administration: stationery, postage, telephones, electronic communications, interlibrary loans

- income generation: fines, photocopying, membership subscriptions, external services and sales of consumables.

3.3.1   Budget allocation

The learning resource service budget may be allocated on a monthly, termly or annual basis. As there is a demand-led element to the allocation, the learning resource service budget may increase, or decrease over the financial year, and may be affected by fluctuations of enrolment, retention and achievement rates, as controlled by the funding councils.

While the funding councils are the major providers of academic institutions' finance, a significant proportion of funds can be derived from other sources, for example, franchised or other collaborative courses, European funding, direct higher education funding to further education colleges, commercial courses or full cost courses. The learning resource service budget should reflect this diversity of income.

3.3.2   Managing the budget

The learning resource manager is accountable for the management of the budget and must be familiar with the parent institution's financial regulations.

The use of budget headings allows the learning resources manager to track expenditure. The finance department of the institution usually allocates headings, but even if it does, it is still wise for the learning resource manager to devise appropriate categories of expenditure.

Learning resource managers will usually have the right to 'vire' funds from one heading to another. This means administering a 'bottom-line' budget, and transferring funds between headings if, and when, necessary. This can be useful in making scarce resources go further, and also in engendering a flexible approach towards resource management, particularly at a time of funding cutbacks. One way of protecting the budget from cutbacks would be to commit acquisitions early on in the year, for example, by paying in advance for standing orders and journal subscriptions.

By far the most complex part of the budget to manage, and the results of which are the most obvious to learning resource users, is the expenditure on acquisitions, that is the allocation of funds to different subject areas or academic departments, and types of material, for example, books, journals, CD-ROMs and electronic materials.

The management of the acquisitions budget includes monitoring the effectiveness of the spend (cost effectiveness), and analysing the patterns of expenditure.

The use of tools such as spreadsheets, databases and acquisition modules will allow the monitoring of expenditure patterns to be carried out, and will help to make any necessary adjustments to expenditure. They will also allow the learning resource manager to provide the management of the institution with appropriate budget information on request.

If changes to expenditure have to be made, these need to be referred back to the operational plan, and particularly to its objectives and performance targets.

Organizational politics have to be taken into account, and, indeed, used to advantage in any approach to resource management within the learning resource service.

Success in managing resources is an art. It is an art of compromise, and rarely, if it is to be successful, one of confrontation. The successful manager has to be credible in terms of 'delivering the goods', however defined by the institution, and at whatever agreed costs.

3.3.3   Income generation

The learning resource service often assists the institution's income generation, for example, by supporting staff in consultancy work and commercial activities and full-cost courses. The learning resource implications of such income-generating activities should be taken into account when fees are calculated, and the learning resource service should receive an appropriate share of such income.

In addition, the learning resource service may engage directly in income generation by selling information services or facilities to external users, by hiring out facilities such as seminar and training rooms, by providing photocopiers and by selling such items as stationery and computer disks.

Collecting fines for overdue materials is also a type of income generation; however, the main reason for fines is to encourage the circulation of stock. This income should be credited to the learning resource service and should not affect its base funding.

3.4   Access

The learning resource service must be accessible to the whole college community and offer a welcoming, friendly and supportive environment. It must cater for a diverse population in terms of age, ability, mode of study and teaching and learning styles.

A growing number of students in further and higher education are not studying on a full-time basis. It is essential that services be flexible enough to cater for their demands. All students, irrespective of their mode of study, are entitled to the full range of services offered by the learning resource service. Senior managers need to be made aware that the learning resource service needs to be able to respond to the needs of all students.

Consideration should be given to:

- Opening hours
  - to be open for all of the teaching day
  - offering weekend and vacation opening where appropriate
- Staff: qualified and adequately trained staff should be available at all times to assist users with their information needs
- Learning materials: the range of learning materials should be diverse and lending services should be flexible and generous to all users
- Access for part time students, distance learners, virtual learners and those on franchised or other collaborative courses
- Access for people with learning difficulties or disabilities: people with learning difficulties or disabilities need access to all facilities. To this end:
  - access should be level
  - there should be lifts between floors and levels
  - OPACs, ICT/ILT and audiovisual equipment should be adapted for visually and hearing impaired users
  - counters, service points, study desks and ICT/ILT workstations should be of suitable height to accommodate users in wheelchairs or with other mobility difficulties
  - there should be enough room for circulation and turning of wheelchairs and spinal carriages
  - there should be a loop system for the hearing impaired
  - signs and guiding should be tactile where possible
  - there should be good use of colour and lighting
  - there should be good acoustics
  - fire alarms should be visible as well as audible
  - properly adapted toilets should be provided
  - Disability Discrimination Act 1995, Health and Safety Executive, Equal Opportunities Commission, British Standards and other guidelines published by relevant national bodies should be adhered to.
- Access to information skills sessions
- Furniture and equipment should be attractive and hard-wearing
- Signs and guiding should be clear and concise enough to encourage users to become more independent.

3.5 Stock

The stock must reflect the teaching and learning needs, as well as the wider information needs, of the institution. The range of learning materials available may take many forms, so the use of the word 'stock' does not refer only to text-based materials. Learning materials should be provided in a variety of formats and styles in order to cater for specific groups.

3.5.1 Size of the collection

Learning resource services must be given an appropriate level of funding annually to enable their collections to reach and maintain the levels of stock necessary to support the curriculum and to enable the purchase of new material to replenish, update and improve stock.

The size of the collection will be further influenced by:

- the number of students
- the size of the institution
- the number of sites on which the learning resource service operates
- the proportion of advanced work
- the proportion of part-time students in the college
- the number of users and potential users of the service
- the subjects taught
- the decisions made as to whether to hold stock or to provide access to collections elsewhere and/or in electronic form
- the resources provided in other areas of the institution
- the modes of course delivery, including managed learning environments
- the storage capacity of the learning resource service.

3.5.2 Stock development

The stock development policy should be based on the information needs and the information strategy of the institution. This policy should specifically address the adequacy of subject cover, which is the primary source of user satisfaction. Other factors include:

- provision for existing courses
- provision for the introduction of new courses
- the number of students
- provision of a range of materials catering for students at all levels of ability on each course
- provision of lending and reference material
- provision of a variety of learning materials to cater for different learning styles
- provision of information to allow institutional managers to make informed decisions
- provision of general and recreational reading material for staff and students
- finance available, with special reference to:

- the price of material in different media
- the price of material in different disciplines
- the proportion of higher-level work
- loss and/or replenishment rates.

3.5.3   Stock management

The learning resource service needs to develop a stock management policy. This policy should identify methods of measuring stock performance in order that decisions can be made about:

- the relevance of current holdings
- where, and how, financial resources should be targeted
- the disposal of materials that have lost their relevance.

A discussion of this topic can be found in the *Library Association Record* article of February 1998, 'Get to know your stock',[12] by George Kerr.

In forming a stock management policy consideration should be given to the following:

- statistics

    Statistics on stock use will provide information that the learning resources manager, in liaison with the teaching staff, can use to make appropriate choices of materials for the collection. These materials can, subsequently, be included on recommended resource lists.

- relevance

    The relevance of materials to the courses provided by the institution and the ability of these materials to be exploited across disciplines should be the key element in their initial purchase. The criteria for discarding stock should be based on the ability of the resources to meet the needs of users.

- replacement

    A learning resource service will require a rolling programme of stock replacement. However, in some disciplines such as computing, law and medicine, the replacement rate will be faster as information in these disciplines changes more quickly. Worn, damaged and obsolescent stock should be replaced regularly.

- stock checks and audits

    A regular programme of stock checks should be established to assess loss and inconsistency. This may be an obligation required by auditors. It has the enhanced benefit of maintaining the currency of the stock and ensuring the accuracy of the catalogue. Heavy losses may indicate the need for improving security measures.

3.5.4   Security

In order to protect stock and to ensure that losses are kept to a minimum, security measures should be carefully considered. Appropriate measures should be taken to secure equipment and guard against theft and damage in learning resource centres. Possible measures include bar-coding, ownership stamps, infra-red security marks, postcode branding, electronic tagging, lockable display cases, equipment clamps and chains.

3.6   Services

The following is a list of services that should be provided as part of a learning resource service. It is not a definitive list, as what is provided will depend on the combination of functions that form a learning resource service.

3.6.1   Study facilities

Study facilities in a learning resource centre should allow for the differing study styles of students and a diversity of teaching and learning methods. There should be areas for silent study, quiet study and group work. The size and shape of a learning resource centre may not lend itself easily to creating these varying environments but the introduction of devices such as acoustic screening can help.

Reconciling the differing study styles of students can be problematic where separation of the environment is not feasible. These tensions are exacerbated by any increase in student numbers. The learning resource manager should work closely with senior management to formulate a solution.

3.6.2   Lending services

The policy for lending materials should be as generous and flexible as possible and the majority of the resources should be available for loan. Users should be able to borrow material in the quantities and for the length of time appropriate to their needs. However, some restrictions may have to be imposed in order to maximize the use of the collection. The introduction of overnight loan and short-term loan collections increases flexibility, but may penalize part time students.

Reservation systems support lending services and ensure the circulation of popular items. Links with outside agencies that provide interlibrary loans will also help to augment collections.

Self-issue and user access to individual records for renewals and reservations, either on site or remotely, are all desirable objectives and increase circulation.

3.6.3   Circulation control

An automated circulation system is imperative for the better control of stock, an improved service to users and enhanced management information. It enables effective, detailed monitoring of loans, informing purchase and disposal decisions. It contributes to early detection of defaulting borrowers, helping to minimize loss.

3.6.4   The catalogue

The catalogue is the key to the collection. An automated catalogue improves the exploitation and analysis of resources and makes it easy for users to identify relevant material.

The catalogue can provide a central record of all learning resources throughout the institution. Therefore it is desirable that the catalogue be available across institutional and external networks. This greatly enhances access and communications. Network and web technology have also made it possible to access the catalogues of an increasingly wide range of external institutions.

3.6.5   Enquiry services

It is desirable that there should be staff with appropriate skills available during the times that the learning resource service is open to advise users on their information needs and to answer enquiries. However, with lengthy opening hours during evenings and at weekends this level of service is not always possible.

If appropriate staff are not immediately available some positive commitment should be made to the user to deal with the question as soon as possible by, for example:

- making an appointment
- making a telephone call
- sending an e-mail
- sending a fax.

The way enquiries are handled is an important aspect of the service and a customer care issue. Therefore suitable training should be regularly undertaken by all levels of learning resource service staff to ensure user satisfaction and a consistent approach.

Learning resource service staff need to think carefully about the positioning of their counters and enquiry desks in order to encourage users to approach and ask questions. Converged services in particular need to think about the level of expertise offered.

Maintaining records of enquiries can be helpful in determining what levels of service need to be provided and what levels of staffing and resources are appropriate.

3.6.6   Information skills and learning support

The learning resource service provides the support that users need to locate, retrieve, select, appraise, organize, record, communicate and evaluate information. It provides an environment in which information skills can be learned, practised and developed.

Every learning resource service should offer a programme of induction and information skills to staff and students. These programmes should be integrated, relevant and at a level and time appropriate to the needs of the user. The information skills programme may form part of a key skills or basic skills curriculum requirement. This could be either qualification based or part of an internal programme.

It should be emphasized that by acquiring information retrieval and evaluation skills students become able to take a greater responsibility for their own lifelong learning. Subject knowledge can change fast. The ability to find information is crucial in the modern world.

The parent institution should recognize that the learning resource staff also have an important support and guidance role, similar to that of their teaching colleagues and other support staff in, for example, student counselling and guidance services.

3.6.7 ICT/ILT

ICT/ILT takes two distinct forms:

- information-based: CD-ROM, online databases, Internet, intranet, DVD, managed learning environments etc
- production-based: word-processing, spreadsheets, PowerPoint presentations, web design and authoring software, CD-ROM production, desktop publishing etc.

Technology should not be introduced without appropriate technical support, staff training or observation of health and safety requirements.

3.6.8 Reprographics

In order to produce assignments to a high standard it may be desirable to introduce more sophisticated photocopying and binding facilities, such as colour and digital copiers, laminators and binding equipment. Where photocopying is carried out copyright laws and licensing agreements should be observed and such guidelines displayed beside the copier.

3.6.9 Audiovisual production

The learning resource service may offer an environment in which audiovisual materials can be produced and edited.

3.6.10 Stationery and materials

The learning resource service can sell stationery and materials such as textbooks, pens, paper and disks.

References

1 Further Education Funding Council, *Guidance on floorspace management in further education colleges: supplement to circular 97/37*, FEFC, 1997.

2 Department for Education, *Accommodation for changes in further education: design note 50*, DES 1994.

3 Further Education Funding Council, op cit.

4 McDonald, A, *Space requirements for academic libraries and learning resource centres*, SCONUL, 1996.

5 Mitchell, D J. (ed), *Library design: principles and practice for the college librarian*, CoFHE, 1992.

6 Mitchell, D J D (ed), *Belfast '96 designs on learning: proceedings of the CoFHE annual study conference held at Stranmillis College, Belfast, 1st-4th April 1996*, CoFHE, 1997.

7 Dadzie, S, *Equality assurance: self-assessment for equal opportunities in further education*, FEDA, 1998.

8 Department for Education, op cit.

9 Further Education Funding Council, op cit.

10 Further Education Funding Council, *Networking lifelong learning: an ILT development strategy for FE*, FEFC, 1999.

11 Brewerton, A, First find some visionaries, *Library Association Record*, **101** (6) June 1999,. 354–6.

12 Kerr, G, Get to know your stock, *Library Association Record*, **100** (2) February 1998, 78–81.

Part 4
Conclusion

Conclusion

The purpose of these *Guidelines* is to describe how a learning resource service should operate, but it is not intended that they should be applied inflexibly. The various sections can be used separately to inform learning resource planning and decision making and to enable learning resource managers to arrive at and justify their decisions.

The document should, however, also be seen as a whole, conveying a standard or set of values about the role and responsibilities of the learning resource service in an academic institution.

A learning resource centre is more than just a collection of learning materials; it is an access point or gateway to a wide range of local, national and international information, and the learning resource staff play a crucial part in connecting users to this information.

Learning resource staff can enhance the learning experience of students; they can add value at the enrolment, on-course and achievement stages of a students programme; they can help to fulfil the information needs and strategy of the institution and they can provide expertise in a range of curriculum and technological initiatives and developments, such as lifelong learning, the Internet, intranets and the Ufi.

Ultimately, the value of these *Guidelines* will lie in their outcomes for users: the satisfaction of users is in the end the raison d'être of a learning resource service and they will be the judges of our work.

Appendices

Appendix I Glossary

This glossary includes general acronyms as well as those used within the text.

AAT	Association of Accounting Technicians
ALF	average level of funding
BECTA	British Educational Communications and Technology Agency
C&G	City and Guilds (of London Institute)
CD-ROM	compact disc–read only memory
CHEST	Combined Higher Education Software Team
CoFHE	Colleges of Further and Higher Education Group (of The Library Association)
CoLRIC	Council for Learning Resources in Colleges
CPD	continuing professional development
CVCP	Committee of Vice-Chancellors and Principals
DENI	Department of Education, Northern Ireland
DES	Department of Education and Science
DfEE	Department for Education and Employment
DVD	digital video disc
EARL	Electronic Access to Resources in Libraries
ETI	Education and Training Inspectorate (of the Department of Education, Northern Ireland)
Estyn	Her Majesty's Inspectorate for Education and Training in Wales
FEDA	Further Education Development Agency
FEFC	Further Education Funding Council
FENC	Further Education National Consortium
FERL	Further Education Resources for Learning
FTE	Full Time Equivalent
HCLRG	Higher Education Funding Councils' Colleges Learning Resources Group
HEFCE	Higher Education Funding Council, England
HEFCW	Higher Education Funding Council, Wales
HESA	Higher Education Statistics Agency
HMI	Her Majesty's Inspectorate
ICT	information and communications technology
ILT	information and learning technology
IIP	Investors in People
IPD	Institute of Personnel and Development
ISO	International Standards Organization
JANET	UK Joint Academic and Research Network
JISC	Joint Information Systems Committee
LAMIT	Multimedia and IT Group (of The Library Association)
LCD	liquid crystal display
LISU	Library and Information Statistics Unit
LRC	learning resource centre

LRDG	Learning Resources Development Group
MLAC	Museums, Libraries,and Archives Council
NIACE	National Institute for Adult and Continuing Education
NVQ	National Vocational Qualification
OFSTED	Office for Standards in Education
OHP	overhead projector
OPAC	online public access catalogue
QAA	Quality Assurance Agency
RBL	resource-based learning
SCONUL	Standing Conference of National and University Libraries
SCOP	Standing Conference of Principals
SHEFC	Scottish Higher Education Funding Council
SPUR	Student Powered Unit of Resource (Northern Ireland)
SUM	Student Unit of Measurement (Scotland)
SVQ	Scottish Vocational Qualification
SWOT	strengths, weaknesses, opportunities and threats
TQA	Teaching Quality Assessment
TQM	total quality management
TTA	Teacher Training Agency
UC&R	University, College and Research Group (of The Library Association)
UCISA	Universities and Colleges Information Systems Association
UKOLN	UK Office for Library and Information Networking
Ufi	University for Industry

A useful glossary of educational acronyms can be found on the FEDA website (see Appendix 8).

Appendix 2   Statistical information

The following statistical data may assist in determining the environmental requirements of a learning resource centre.

Allocation of college space [1]
The total area for further education college learning resource centres should be:

- at least 10% of total college area or
- a minimum of 20% of the total teaching space.

Load bearing structure [2]
The load bearing capacity of the floor housing books stacks must exceed a minimum strength of 6.5 kNm^{-2}.

Light [3]
50% daylight is recommended, but the glare of the sun must be cut out.

Lighting [4]
- Work surfaces should receive minimum illumination of 300 Lux
- Light fittings should produce a glare index no higher than 19.

Heating [5]
The minimum temperature should be 18°C when the external air temperature is –1°C.

Ventilation [6]
- minimum ventilation should be at least 3 litres of fresh air per second per occupant
- capability should exist of providing at least 8 litres of fresh air per second per occupant on very hot days
- natural ventilation is preferred; mechanical methods should be draught free.

Allocation of learning resource centre space [7]

Number of students	Floor area, m^2			
	Book stacks	Desk/workspace	Study/periodicals	Total area
250 FTE	50	70	63	183
1000 FTE	138	95	250	483
3000 FTE	338	155	750	1243

Study space
- 1 seat per 10 students FTE in further education [8]
- 1 seat per 6 students FTE in higher education [9]
- 2.5 m^2 per student workspace in resource-based learning rooms or learning resource centres [10]

- between 2.5 m² and 4 m² per student workspace in higher education[11]
- reader modules minimum 900mm x 600mm[12]
- ICT/ILT spaces minimum 1200mm x 800mm.[13]

References

1 Further Education Funding Council, *Guidance on floorspace management in further education colleges: supplement to circular 97/37*, FEFC, 1997.

2 McDonald, A, *Moving your learning resource service*, Aslib, 1994.

3 Rogers, L, New British libraries: sector report learning resource centres, *Royal Institute of British Architects: Interiors*, October, 1995.

4 Department for Education and Employment, *Structural requirements and health and safety: circular no.10/96*, DfEE, 1996.

5 Department for Education and Employment, ibid.

6 Department for Education and Employment, ibid.

7 Department of Education and Science, *Area guidelines for sixth form, tertiary and NAFE colleges: design note 33*, DES, 1983.

8 Department of Education and Science, ibid.

9 Joint Funding Councils' Libraries Review Group, *Report: a report for the HEFCE, SHEFC, HEFCW and DENI (Follett)*, HEFC, 1993.

10 Further Education Funding Council, *Accommodation strategies: guidance for colleges: supplement to circular 97/19*, FEFC, 1997.

11 McDonald, A, *Space requirements for academic libraries and learning resource centre*, SCONUL, 1996.

12 Joint Funding Councils' Libraries Review Group, op cit.

13 Joint Funding Councils' Libraries Review Group, op cit

Appendix 3 Management data checklist

This management data checklist was prepared by Roddie Shepherd, The Library Association's Professional Adviser (Academic), April 1999.

Quantitative data (efficiency)

Resources (inputs)

Physical
- Floor area/FTE student
- Floor area/registered user
- Study places/FTE student
- Study places/registered user
- Books/FTE student
- Books/registered user
- Multimedia/FTE student
- Multimedia/registered user
- CD-ROM licences/FTE student
- CD-ROM licences/registered user
- Software licences/FTE student
- Software licences/registered user
- Periodical subs/FTE student
- Periodical subs/registered user

ICT/ILT
- Student access terminals/FTE student
- Student access terminals/registered user
- Computer workstations/FTE student
- Computer workstations/registered user
- CD-ROM workstations/FTE student
- CD-ROM workstations/registered user
- Internet workstations/FTE student
- Internet workstations/registered user

Human
- FTE learning resource staff/FTE student
- FTE learning resource staff/registered user
- FTE professional learning resource staff/FTE student
- FTE professional learning resource staff/registered user
- FTE learning resource staff/FTE teaching staff

Financial
- Total service budget/FTE student

- Total service budget/registered user
- Staff budget/FTE student
- Staff budget/registered user
- Staff budget as a percentage of total service budget
- Staff development budget/member of staff
- Staff development budget as a percentage of total service budget
- Learning materials and services budget (bookfund)/FTE student
- Learning materials and services budget (bookfund)/registered user
- Learning materials and services budget (bookfund) as a percentage of total service budget
- Equipment and stationery budget/FTE student
- Equipment and stationery budget/registered user
- Equipment and stationery budget as a percentage of total service budget
- Automation budget/FTE student
- Automation budget/registered user
- Automation budget as a percentage of total service budget
- Capital allocation/FTE student
- Capital allocation/registered user

Time (Accessibility)

- Opening hours/term time week/FTE learning resource staff
- Opening hours/vacation time week/FTE learning resource staff

Processes (throughputs)

User education

- Number of hours/FTE student
- Percentage of eligible students attending at least one session

Curriculum liaison

- Number of course team meetings attended/curriculum area

Income

- Total income generated per annum as a percentage of revenue budget

Learning resources maintenance

- Items added/FTE student
- Items added as a percentage of stock base
- Items withdrawn as a percentage of stock base

Learning resources supply

- Percentage of items available for loan within, for example:
  - 8 weeks of order
  - 12 weeks of order
  - 16 weeks of order

Learning resources losses

- Value of items lost from stock per annum as a percentage of bookfund

Interlibrary loans

- Percentage of items obtained from external sources supplied within, for example:
  - 2 weeks of request
  - 4 weeks of request
  - 6 weeks of request

Utilization (outputs)

Market penetration

- Percentage of eligible students registered with the learning resource service
- Percentage of eligible staff registered with the learning resource service
- Percentage of eligible students who are active users of the learning resource service
- Percentage of eligible staff who are active users of the learning resource service

Time utilization

- Average occupancy/hours of opening
- Median occupancy/hours of opening

Space utilization

- Average occupancy/hours of opening as a percentage of study places
- Median occupancy/hour of opening as a percentage of study places

Learning resources utilization

- Annual issues/item of stock
- Annual issues/FTE student
- Annual issues/registered user
- Annual log-ons/licence
- Annual log-ons/FTE student
- Annual log-ons/registered user
- Annual net searches/FTE student
- Annual net searches/registered user

Enquiries

- Number of substantial enquiries (over 5 minutes)/FTE student
- Number of substantial enquiries (over 5 minutes)/registered user

Workstation utilization

- Average occupancy computers/term time
- Median occupancy computers/term time
- Average occupancy computers/hours of opening as a percentage of computers available

- Median occupancy computers/hours of opening as a percentage of computers available

Non-routine data collection

- Document availability (hit rate)
- Intensity of use of stock by subject area (average number of times an item is borrowed per annum)
- Percentage of new items borrowed or accessed within a year of purchase
- Items consulted but not borrowed
- Percentage of total stock borrowed or consulted per annum
- New items supply time survey
- Age profile of learning resources in selected subject areas
- Usage of periodical titles
- Requests or interlibrary loans surveys

Costs

- Unit cost of the service (ie revenue cost per FTE enrolled student)
- Unit cost/registered user
- Unit cost/opening hours
- Unit cost/study places

Environmental indicators

- Average price/item acquired by category of material (eg software licence, CD-ROM subscriptions, book, periodical)
- Median price/items acquired by category of material
- Learning resources price inflation by category of material (college purchase, national)
- College students, FTE
- College students, numbers
- College funding units
- Student recruitment (percentage increase or decrease)

Qualitative data (effectiveness)

- Focus group consultation: small group, open discussion, loose agenda
- Attitude survey: large-scale, questionnaire, mainly closed questions, representative sample
- Success of visit survey
- Special group survey, for example, part-time students; evening students
- Special purpose survey, for example, opening hours
- User education session evaluation forms
- Suggestions book or box
- Complaints procedure
- Faculty Board/Course Team/Campus Council meetings
- Inspectors' and Assessors' reports

- Peer review
- Library staff appraisal
- Library staff survey

Appendix 4 The Role of The Library Association

The Library Association was founded on 5 October 1877. Twenty-one years later, on 17 February 1898, Queen Victoria granted The Association a Royal Charter.

In 1986, Queen Elizabeth II granted a Supplemental Charter which amended the purposes and powers in the original Charter to reflect The Association's contemporary role. These purposes and powers are as follows:

1 To represent and act as the professional body for persons working in or interested in library and information services.
2 To scrutinize any legislation affecting the provision of library and information services and to promote such further legislation as may be considered necessary to this end.
3 To promote and encourage the maintenance of adequate and appropriate provision of library and information services of various kinds throughout the United Kingdom, the Channel Islands and the Isle of Man.
4 To promote the better management of library and information services.
5 To promote the improvement of the knowledge, skills, position and qualifications of librarians and information personnel.
6 To maintain a register of Chartered Members, qualified to practise as professional librarians and information personnel.
7 To promote study and research in librarianship and information science and to disseminate the results.
8 To ensure the effective dissemination of appropriate information of interest to members.
9 To work with similar associations overseas with appropriate international bodies to promote the widespread provision of adequate and appropriate library and information services.
10 To provide appropriate services to members in furtherance of these objectives.
11 To do all such lawful things as are incidental or conducive to the attainment of the above objects.

The Library Association is organized into 12 regional Branches, one of which all members automatically join; and 22 Special Interest Groups (of which CoFHE is one) which members may opt to join.

Appendix 5   The Role of the Professional Adviser (Academic)

The Professional Adviser (Academic) is a member of the Professional Advisory Team at The Library Association. There are five professional posts in this team: one each for public library services, youth and school library services, and for academic library services; and two for workplace library services. The Professional Adviser (Academic) is the leading Library Association officer on library and information services in further and higher education, and on adult learning and library and information services.

The main elements of the role of the Professional Adviser (Academic) post are:

1   **Advocacy and representation of the contribution of librarians and libraries**
This takes the form of, for example:

   - responses and submissions to government; planning, funding and quality assurance agencies; and other policy bodies
   - meetings with policy advisers and representatives of government and other agencies involved in education and learning
   - representations to individual institutions.

2   **Provision of advice and support to individual practitioners in the sector**
This covers a wide range of professional, managerial and employment-related issues. It can take the form of direct advice, or of referral to colleagues in the field who have relevant experience that they are willing to share. The pool of expertise represented in the professional advisory team is a valuable resource on which practitioners can draw.

3   **Dissemination of good practice, innovation and policy awareness**
Typically this takes the form of presentations and workshops, contributing to the planning and design of conferences and CPD events, publication and commissioning of articles, use of websites and e-lists, and of professional visits and liaison work.

4   **Development of professional policy and practice**
This involves, for example, the instigation of research projects, contributing to the compilation of Library Association guidelines, and carrying forward the work of The Library Association's Academic and Research Libraries Committee and Adult Learning and Libraries Sub-Committee.

The Professional Adviser (Academic) is the designated liaison officer at Library Association Headquarters for the CoFHE and UC&R special interest groups.

Appendix 6 The Library Association's Code of Professional Conduct

Preface to The Library Association's Code of Professional Conduct

Why have a Code?

The Code of Conduct indicates the standards of behaviour expected of a member of The Association. It sets out, in general terms, the standards and duties which it is reasonable to expect a professional to observe. This can be used as a point of reference when dealing with disciplinary procedures against members. This is intended to protect the profession, individual practitioners, and their clients.

If you have a complaint

Complaints under the Code of Professional Conduct or the Bye-laws of The Library Association may be made by anybody, whether they are members of The Association or not. If you believe you have such a complaint, please write, in confidence to: The Chief Executive, The Library Association, 7 Ridgmount Street, London WC1E 7AE.

The Chief Executive will consider the complaint and seek the advice of the Disciplinary Committee's advisory panel before deciding to refer it to the full Disciplinary Committee of Library Association Council. Those complaints that are upheld following rigorous investigation may result in expulsion, suspension, reprimand, admonition and guidance on future behaviour.

Additional advice

We are happy to answer any queries concerning this document. If there is any section that you would like clarifying further, please contact The Library Association Chief Executive.

This Code of Professional Conduct was approved by Library Association Council and the Annual General Meeting in 1983, in accordance with The Library Association's Bye-law 45(a).

Please note the term 'librarian' throughout this document includes all library and information personnel, however styled.

A set of guidance notes on the Code is available on request from Information Services.

The Library Association's Code of Professional Conduct

1 Members of The Association must conduct themselves in such a way that their conduct would not be reasonably regarded by their professional colleagues within the field of librarianship (including the provision of information services) as

serious professional misconduct or as professional misconduct. It is by this over-all test that the conduct will be judged.

2a Members must comply with the Charter and Bye-laws of The Association and the provisions of this Code of Conduct;

b Members must not engage in conduct which may seriously prejudice the standing and reputation of the library profession or of The Library Association.

c Members must be competent in their professional activities including the requirement:

i to keep abreast of developments in librarianship in those branches of professional practice in which qualifications and experience entitle them to engage;

ii in respect of those members of the Association responsible for supervising the training and duties of another librarian, to ensure that those whom they supervise are trained to carry out their duties in a competent manner.

d Members' primary duty when acting in the capacity of librarian is to their clients, ie the persons or groups of persons for whose requirements and use are intended the resources and services which the members are engaged to provide. In all professional considerations the interests of the clients within their prescribed or legitimate requirements take precedence over all other interests. It is recognized that the persons or groups of persons to whom this duty is owed will vary according to the nature of the employment which members undertake. In particular it is recognized that different considerations will apply where members are working at a place to which the public has right of access from those where they are working in an environment where the public is excluded or given only limited access.

e In places to which the public has right of access, save where the flow of information must be restricted by reason of confidentiality, members have an obligation to facilitate the flow of information and ideas and to protect and promote the rights of every individual to have free and equal access to sources of information without discrimination and within the limits of the law.

f Members must fulfil to the best of their ability the contractual obligations owed to their employer. However circumstances may arise when the public interest or the reputation of the profession itself may be at variance with the narrower interests of an employer. If it is found to be impossible to reconcile such difference then public interest and the maintenance of professional standards must be the primary considerations.

g Members should not knowingly promote material the prime purpose of which is to encourage discrimination on the grounds of race, colour, creed, gender or sexual orientation. It shall not be regarded as promoting such material to divulge it for the purpose of studying the subject of that discrimination.

h (i) Members must not divulge or permit to be divulged any materials, information or administrative record (in manual or electronic form) which has been entrusted to them in confidence, to any third party nor use such information without the prior consent of the client for any purpose other than that for which it was first obtained. This duty to the client continues after the relationship of librarian and client ceases.

(ii) Members are absolved from the duty set out in sub-paragraph (i) above in so far as is required by law and in so far as it is necessary to answer accusations before the Disciplinary Committee.

i Members' actions and decisions should be determined solely by their professional judgement and they should not profit from their position otherwise than by normal remuneration or fee for professional services.

j Members must report the facts to the Secretary of The Library Association if convicted of any offence involving dishonesty or one which brings the profession into disrepute.

k Members must:

(i) respond to any requirements from the Disciplinary Committee for comments or information on a complaint;

(ii) attend the committee proceedings when required to do so, with such representation as is provided for in the Bye-Laws;

(iii) attend upon a nominated person for the purpose of receiving guidance as to future conduct if required to do so.

3a Failure to comply with the requirements set out in paragraph 2, including the requirements relating to competence may, if proved before the Disciplinary Committee be regarded by it as serious professional misconduct and, if so, shall render the member concerned liable to be expelled or suspended (either unconditionally or subject to conditions) to be ordered to repay or forego fees and expenses as appropriate, or to be reprimanded and/or to be ordered to pay the costs of the hearing.

b Failure to comply with the requirements set out in paragraph 2, which, in the opinion of the Disciplinary Committee, falls short of serious professional misconduct may, if proved, render the member liable to be admonished or to be given appropriate guidance as to his or her future conduct.

c The provisions of Bye-Laws 44–46 shall apply.

Appendix 7   Useful publications

Design

Harrison, D (ed), *Library buildings 1990-1994*, Library Services Ltd, 1995.

Hawthorne, P, *Planning additions to academic library buildings*, American Library Association, 1995.

Holt, R M, *Planning library buildings and facilities: from concept to completion*, Scarecrow, 1989.

Leighton, P and Weber, D C, *Planning academic and research library buildings*, American Library Association, 1999.

Sykes, J, *Choosing library furniture*, SCONUL, 1998.

Financial management

Baker, D, *Resource management in academic libraries*, Library Association Publishing, 1997.

Franchised and other collaborative courses

The Library Association, *Library and learning resource provision for franchised and other collaborative courses* (Guideline), The Library Association, 1999.

Health and safety

Health and Safety Executive, *A guide to risk assessment requirements*, HSE, 1966.

Health and Safety Executive, *Five steps to risk assessment*, HSE, 1998.

MSF Health and Safety, *Work with display screen equipment: a guide to health and safety*, MSF Health and Safety Information No. 38, 1993.

Information skills

Johnson, H, An information skills model: do we need one?, *SCONUL Newsletter*, Autumn 1999.

Mitchell, D J D (ed), *Edinburgh '95: serving our students: information skills for the new millennium: papers presented at the CoFHE annual study conference held at Pollock Halls, University of Edinburgh, 10th-13th April 1995*, CoFHE, 1996.

Warrington, S R (ed), *Exeter '97: virtual libraries, virtual librarians: proceedings of the CoFHE annual study conference held at the University of Exeter, 24th-27th March 1997*, CoFHE, 1998.

Inspection and assessment

Further Education Funding Council, *Annual report 1998-99: delivering the new agenda*, FEFC, 1999.

Further Education Funding Council, *Validating self-assessment: circular 97/12*, FEFC, 1997.

Further Education Funding Council, *Self-assessment and inspection: circular 97/13*, FEFC 1997.

Marketing

Pantry, S and Griffiths, P, *Becoming a successful intrapreneur: a practical guide to creating an innovative information service*, Library Association Publishing, 1998.

Performance measurement

Bloor, I, *Performance indicators and decision support systems for libraries: British Library Research Paper 93*, British Library Research and Development Department, 1991.

British Standards Institution, *BS ISO 11620: information and documentation: library performance indicators*, BSI, 1998.

Higher Education Funding Council for England et al, *The effective academic library: a framework for evaluating the performance of UK academic libraries: a consultative report to the HEFCE, SHEFC, HEFCW and DENI by the Joint Funding Councils' ad-hoc group on performance indicators for libraries*, HEFCE, 1995.

Lancaster, F W, *If you want to evaluate your library . . .* , 2nd edn, University of Illinois and Library Association Publishing, 1993.

Morgan, S, *Performance measurement in academic libraries*, Mansell, 1995.

Van House, N A. et al, *Measuring academic library performance: a practical approach: prepared for the Association of College and Research Libraries ad-hoc committee on performance measures*, American Library Association, 1990.

Statistics

Creaser, C and Murphy, A, *LISU annual library statistics*, 1999, LIC Research Report 21, 1999.

Hamm, T, et. al, *Resources for learning in college libraries: the report of the LA College Library Survey 1993–94*, Library Association Publishing, 1995.

Higher Education Funding Council Colleges Learning Resources Group, *Annual statistics*, HCLRG (annual).

Spiller, D (ed), *Academic library surveys and statistics in practice: proceedings of a seminar held at Loughborough University 2–3 June 1997: LISU Occasional Paper no. 16*, LISU, 1998.

Standing Conference of National and University Libraries, *Annual library statistics*, SCONUL (annual).

Standing Conference of National and University Libraries and Higher Education Funding Council Colleges Learning Resources Group, *UK higher education library management statistics 1997–98*, SCONUL/HCLRG, 1999.

Strategic management

Corrall, S, *Strategic planning for library and information services: Aslib know how guide*, 2nd edn, Aslib, 2000.

Other

Council for Learning Resources in Colleges, *Working paper (various titles: charters, job descriptions for learning resources assistants; job descriptions for learning resources deputies; job descriptions for learning resources managers; organisational structures; policies and procedures; service level agreements; strategic plans)*, CoLRIC, 1999.

Scottish Library and Information Council, *Libraries in Scottish further education colleges: standards for performance and resourcing*, Scottish Library and Information Council, 1997.

Appendix 8   Useful websites

Library associations and associated groups

CoFHE	http://www.la-hq.org.uk/groups/cofhe/cofhe.html
CoLRIC	http://www.colric.org.uk
The Library Association	http://www.la-hq.org.uk
NEC	http://www.nec.ac.uk
SCONUL	http://www.sconul.ac.uk
Scottish Library Association	http://www.slainte.org.uk
UC&R	http://www.ucrg.ogr.uk
Welsh Library Association	http://www.llgc.org.uk/wla/

Further education/higher education sites

Academic Directory	http://acdc.hensa.ac.uk/
CVCP	http://www.cvcp.ac.uk/
DENI	http://www.nics.gov.uk/
DfEE	http://www.dfee.gov.uk/
FEDA	http://www.feda.ac.uk/
FEFC	http://www.fefc.ac.uk/
FENC	http://www.fenc.org.uk/
HEFCE	http://www.hefce.ac.uk/
HEFCW	http://www.wfc.ac.uk
HESA	http://www.hesa.ac.uk
NIACE	http://www.niace.org.uk
OFSTED	http://www.ofsted.gov.uk/
QAA	http://www.niss.ac.uk/education/qaa/
SCOP	http://www.scop.ac.uk/
SHEFC	http://www.shefc.ac.uk/shefc/welcome.htm
TTA	http://www.teach-tta.gov.uk
UCAS	http://www.ucas.ac.uk/
UCISA	http://www.ucisa.ac.uk/
UK FE, HE and University Colleges	http://www.bham.ac.uk/webmaster/ukcwww.html
UK Higher Education and Research Libraries	http://www.ex.ac.uk/library/uklibs.html
UK Lifelong Learning	http://www.lifelonglearning.co.uk/
UK Sensitive Maps	http://www.scit.wlv.ac.uk/ukinfo/uk.map.html

Information and technology sites

BECTA	http://www.becta.org.uk/
CHEST	http://www.chest.ac.uk/

EARL	http://www.earl.org.uk/
FERL	http//ferl.becta.org.uk/
JANET	http://www.ja.net/
JISC	http://www.jisc.ac.uk/
UKOLN	http://www.ukoln.ac.uk/

Government Information

| CCTA Government Information Service | http://www.open.gov.uk/ |

Bibliography

Brewerton, A, First, find some visionaries, *Library Association Record*, **101** (6) June 1999, 354–6.

Council for Learning Resources in Colleges, *Guidelines for inspection of college libraries/learning resource services*, CoLRIC, 1993.

Dadzie, S, *Equality assurance: self-assessment for equal opportunities in further education*, FEDA, 1998.

Department For Education, *Accommodation for changes in further education: Design Note 50*, DFE, 1994.

Department for Education and Employment, *Structural requirements and health and safety: circular no. 10/96*, DfEE, 1996.

Department of Education and Science, *Area guidelines for sixth form, tertiary and NAFE colleges: design note 33*, DES, 1983.

Further Education Funding Council, *Accommodation strategies: guidance for colleges: supplement to Circular 97/19*, FEFC, 1997.

Further Education Funding Council, *Guidance on floorspace management in further education colleges: supplement to circular 97/37*, FEFC, 1997.

Further Education Funding Council, *Networking lifelong learning: an ILT development strategy for FE*, FEFC, 1999.

Hannagan, T, *Management: concepts and practices*, Financial Times Management, 1998.

Higher Education Funding Council for England: Quality Assessment Division, *Assessor's handbook*, HEFCE, 1996.

Joint Funding Councils' Libraries Review Group, *Report: a report for the HEFCE, SHEFC, HEFCW and DENI (Follett)*, HEFC, 1993.

Kerr, G, Get to know your stock, *Library Association Record*, **100** (2) February 1998, 78–81.

McDonald, A, *Moving your learning resource service*, Aslib, 1994.

McDonald, A, *Space requirements for academic libraries and learning resource centre*, SCONUL, 1996.

Mitchell, D J D (ed), *Belfast '96: designs on learning: proceedings of the CoFHE annual study conference held at Stranmillis College, Belfast, 1st–4th April 1996*, CoFHE, 1997.

Mitchell, D J (ed), *Library design: principles and practice for the college librarian*, CoFHE, 1992.

Rogers, L, New British libraries: sector report learning resource centres, *Royal Institute of British Architects: Interiors*, October 1995.

Standing Conference of National and University Libraries, *Aide-memoire for assessors when evaluating library and computing services*, SCONUL, 1996.

Streatfield, D and Markless, S, *The effective college library*, FEDA, 1997.

Wallace, W and Marsden, D, *Library and learning resource services in further education: the report of the 1996/97 survey commissioned by The Library Association*, The Survey and Statistical Research Centre, Sheffield Hallam University, 1999.

Index

Please note that the numbers refer to part and section numbers, not page numbers